IMPORTANT EVENTS IN HISTORY

The Battle of Hastings

Helen Cox Cannons

raintree

Raintree is an imprint of Capstone Global Library Limited, a company incorporated in England and Wales having its registered office at 264 Banbury Road, Oxford, OX2 7DY – Registered company number: 6695582

www.raintree.co.uk
myorders@raintree.co.uk

Edited by Clare Lewis
Designed by Steve Mead
Picture research by Kelly Garvin
Production by Helen McCreath
Originated by Capstone Global Library
Printed and bound in China

ISBN 978 1 4747 1437 2 (hardback)
19 18 17 16 15
10 9 8 7 6 5 4 3 2 1

ISBN 978 1 4747 1448 8 (paperback)
20 19 18 17 16
10 9 8 7 6 5 4 3 2 1

British Library Cataloguing in Publication Data
A full catalogue record for this book is available from the British Library.

Acknowledgements
We would like to thank the following for permission to reproduce images: Alamy: 19th era, 12, World History Archive, 13; Bridgeman Images: Private Collection/© Look and Learn/The Battle of Hastings, English School, (20th century), 5, Private Collection/(c)Look and Learn/The Battle of Hastings, Nicolle, Pat (Patrick) (1907-95), 17; Capstone Press: Ron Tiner, back cover, 14, 15, 16; Getty Images: AFP/Carl de Souza, 19, Duncan Walker, 11, Hulton Archive, 8, Hulton Archive/The Print Collector, 7, Lonely Planet Images/Simon Greenwood, 18, Oli Scarff, cover (re-enactment); Newscom: akg-images/British Library, 6, CMSP Education, 20, Ingram Publishing, 10, Robert Harding/Walter Rawlings, 22, Ron Sachs - CNP, 21, World History Archive, 9; Shutterstock: Artindo, 4, jorisvo, cover (Bayeux Tapestry)
Design Elements
Shutterstock: LiliGraphie, Osipovfoto

Every effort has been made to contact copyright holders of material reproduced in this book. Any omissions will be rectified in subsequent printings if notice is given to the publisher.

All the internet addresses (URLs) given in this book were valid at the time of going to press. However, due to the dynamic nature of the internet, some addresses may have changed, or sites may have changed or ceased to exist since publication. While the author and publisher regret any inconvenience this may cause readers, no responsibility for any such changes can be accepted by either the author or the publisher.

Contents

Some words are shown in bold, **like this.** You can find out what they mean by looking in the glossary.

What was the Battle of Hastings?

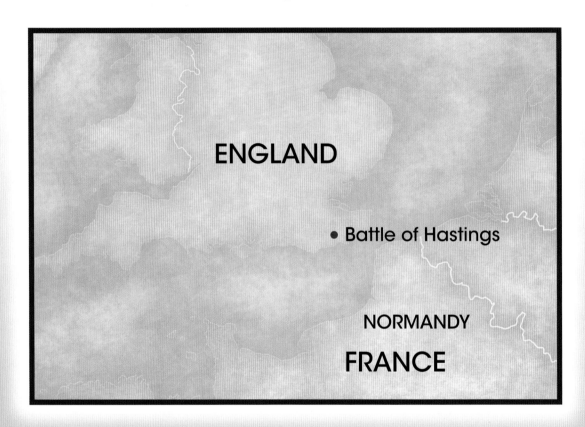

ENGLAND

• Battle of Hastings

NORMANDY

FRANCE

On 14 October 1066, an important battle took place near Hastings in the south of England. It became known as the Battle of Hastings.

The battle was between the armies of two men who both wanted to be the new King of England. This is the true story of the Battle of Hastings.

Who was King at the start of 1066?

As the year of 1066 began, Edward the Confessor was King of England. He was an **Anglo-Saxon** king. The Anglo-Saxons had ruled England for 500 years.

When he was young, Edward and his family had lived in Normandy, in France. As King of England, Edward had French **Normans** in his court. The rich and powerful **earls** of England did not like Edward having Normans at court.

Who was Harold Godwinson?

Harold Godwinson was the **Earl** of Essex. He was the second-most powerful man in England, after the king.

Harold was a brave, strong soldier.
King Edward told everyone he wanted
Harold to be king after him.

Who was William, Duke of Normandy?

William, Duke of Normandy, was King Edward's cousin. The two men knew each other well. William was strong, brave in battle and **ambitious**.

In 1064, William helped Harold Godwinson when Harold's ship was wrecked near France. In return, Harold promised to be loyal to William. William believed that Harold would help him to become King of England one day.

How did Harold become king?

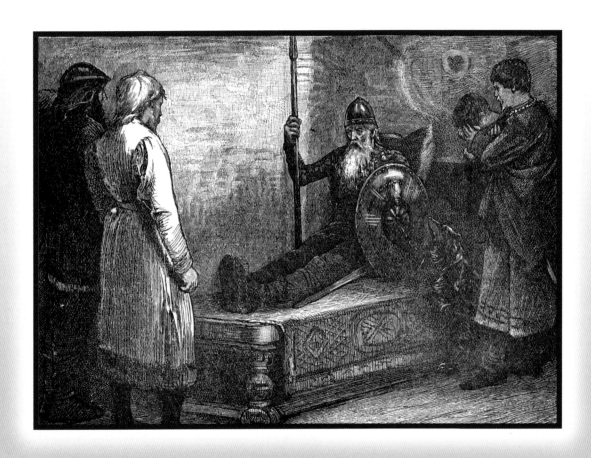

On 5 January 1066, Edward the Confessor died. The **earls** wanted the next king to be English. They did not want a French king.

So, the earls crowned Harold the King of England the very next day. When William heard the news, he was furious.

What did William do?

William got his mighty **Norman** army together and sailed from France to England. He was determined to be King. William's men landed near Hastings, in the south of England.

When the Norman army landed in the
south of England, Harold was in the north.
He and his **Anglo-Saxon** army were fighting
Harald Hardrada, King of Norway. Hardrada
also wanted to be King of England.

How did the Battle of Hastings begin?

Harold and his army **defeated** Hardrada and quickly marched south to fight the **Normans**. By the time they met William's army at Hastings they were tired from fighting and marching.

Harold's **Anglo-Saxon** army started at the top of Senlac Hill. Being above the enemy was a good battle position. William's Norman army were at the bottom of the hill. But William's army was well-trained with expert **archers**.

How did the battle end?

battle re-enactment

The battle was fierce and many soldiers were injured. William's archers fired many arrows but Harold's **Anglo-Saxons** had shields to hold up in **defence**. The fighting went on all day.

battle re-enactment

William's strong, well-trained **Norman** army were proving tough to beat. Harold's wall of shields started to break apart. Suddenly, one of William's **archers** shot an arrow straight into Harold's eye. Harold was dead.

How did William become King?

William was crowned King of England on Christmas Day, 1066. He became known as William the **Conqueror**. The rule of the **Anglo-Saxons** was now over. William went on to rule England for 21 years.

William and the French kings who came after him changed how England was run. They made the English people use the French language. There are many **Norman** castles and cathedrals from William's reign still standing today, including the Tower of London.

What is the Bayeux Tapestry?

The Bayeux Tapestry is a giant piece of **embroidery**. It tells the story of the Battle of Hastings. It is believed to have been  made in Normandy in the late 11th century. The most famous scene in the tapestry is of Harold being hit in the eye by an arrow.

Glossary

ambitious wanting to do well and succeed

Anglo-Saxon English people who had ruled and lived in England for many years

archer soldier who fires arrows from a bow

conqueror someone who wins against enemies in battle

defeat beat in battle

defence protection from harm

earl rich and powerful English man

embroidery pattern or picture stitched onto cloth

Norman from Normandy. Normandy is an area in France.

Find out more

The Anglo-Saxons (Britain in the Past),
  Moira Butterfield (Franklin Watts, 2015)
The Battle of Hastings (Great Events),
  Gillian Clements (Franklin Watts, 2014)

Index